NEW YORK

PHOTOGRAPHS BY LANCE LENSFIELD

teNeues

To Mary

Andre Gide once observed that to write about a place you should be there for two weeks or for twenty years and maybe this is also true of photographers. Some seem as at home with the scenes they photograph as a log with the forest floor or a prisoner with his cell. Others zero in on their targets, like fresh arrivals, sharp-eyed and astonished, looking at the familiar and making it new. That is the strategy of Lance Lensfield.

That is just as it should be because "Lance Lensfield" actually is a fresh arrival. He is the alter ego of Stefan May, who is well-known for sensual pictures shot both in color and black & white with medium-size cameras. Lance Lensfield sprang into being for just this project: A picture-book of New York, shot in black & white, using small format cameras, like Leicas. He visited the city for the first time in 1995, came back annually for a couple of days, a week, or two weeks, and the book took shape. Then came September 11. Lensfield had three choices. He decided that ignoring the event was impossible and that concentrating on it exclusively was not to his taste. So we have what we see here.

We begin looking down vertiginously on the old-fashioned futurity of the cityscape, as if from a small plane, then we swoop down on a woman, her naked back gleaming like a seal, as she herself looks down – from a hotel room, judging by the unmade bed. Soon we are on a subway, a street that explodes like shellfire, a medley of citizens and, suddenly, the World Trade Center as huge and simple as a kid's toy.

Do I seem to be describing a movie? To this eye the book is paced like a movie. People, cars, buildings swoosh towards us, and past, always hinting at a story. Consider the giant human figure, that seems to be reflected on the side of a skyscraper, as though about to break into it, or burst out, and the way that neons bloom, clouds float and the Twin Towers appear again, exploding into wriggling worms of ecstatic light. This city lives, pumping like a heart, vibrating like a nervous system, working like a brain.

Yet another picture of the Twin Towers shows them evanescent as though made of paper, glimpsed through the arch on Washington Square. Beside this image is another. The Towers are soaring confident-

ly, apparently to the moon, actually to an explosion of camera-created light. But then a picture of a sign reading: NEW YORK – TOUGHEST CITY ON EARTH is appropriately ominous. It precedes a gut-wrenching photograph of Ground Zero – an image with a haunting resemblance to a Tower of Babel by a Pieter Breughel, but fallen, and metastised into twisted iron. In another picture shot through the arch on Washington Square – an image which carries a charge at odds with its tranquil bustle – the Twin Towers are gone. Other pictures show the signs that sprouted shortly thereafter like blossoms. The last two images in the book show the Statue of Liberty, spectral but dominant, and a young couple, arm in arm, striding through the traffic the way New Yorkers do. The story continues. That is the story.

But there is another story too. It is hard to photograph New York – a city rivaled only by Paris and Venice in the number of times it has appeared in movies, on TV, in advertisements and on a gadzillion postcards. Lensfield has taken some shots of appropriate landmarks – the Flatiron Building, reflected in a puddle, the Chrysler, blobby in an office window above a Coca Cola truck, Harlem's Cotton Club, the debonair statuary at the Rockefeller Center, the cathedral-like central space of Grand Central Station – but leafing through these images of high buildings, bright nocturnal lights, the kaleidoscope of the faces on the sidewalks, I found again the city that had exhiliarated me when I moved here almost a quarter of a century ago, but which I had stopped really noticing, as you do with the overly familiar. And now here it was again – fresh as a bucketful of ice-water in the face. This is what New York looks like to new eyes.

Anthony Haden-Guest

André Gide bemerkte einmal, man müsse, um über einen Ort zu schreiben, dort zwei Wochen oder aber zwanzig Jahre gelebt haben. Vielleicht gilt das auch für Fotografen. Manche von ihnen scheinen mit dem, was sie fotografieren, so vertraut zu sein wie ein Baumstamm mit dem Waldboden oder ein Häftling mit seiner Zelle. Andere nehmen ihre Motive wie Neuankömmlinge ins Visier. Mit scharfen Augen und staunend betrachten sie das längst Vertraute und zeigen es in neuem Licht. Das ist die Methode von Lance Lensfield.

Und das ist genau so wie es sein sollte. Denn "Lance Lensfield" ist selbst ein Neuankömmling. Er ist das andere Ich von Stefan May, der für seine sinnlichen, mit Mittelformatkameras aufgenommenen Farb- und Schwarzweißbilder bekannt ist. Lance Lensfield wurde eigens durch dieses Projekt ins Leben gerufen: ein Buch mit Bildern von New York, aufgenommen in Schwarzweiß mit Leica-Kleinbildkameras. Er besuchte die Stadt zum ersten Mal 1995, kehrte dann jedes Jahr für einige Tage oder auch ein, zwei Wochen zurück, und allmählich nahm das Buch Gestalt an. Dann kam der 11. September. Lensfield hatte drei Optionen. Das Ereignis zu ignorieren war ihm nicht möglich, sich ausschließlich darauf zu konzentrieren entsprach nicht seiner Art. So entstand, was jetzt vor uns liegt.

Wir beginnen mit einem Schwindel erregenden Blick, als befänden wir uns in einem kleinen Flugzeug, auf die seltsam altmodische und doch futuristische Landschaft der Stadt. Danach schwenken wir hinab auf eine Frau, deren nackter Rücken wie Seehundsfell schimmert, während sie ihrerseits – aus einem Hotelzimmer, wie das ungemachte Bett vermuten lässt – nach unten schaut. Bald finden wir uns in einer U-Bahn wieder, dann in einer Straße, die zu explodieren scheint, wir begegnen den verschiedensten Bewohnern der Stadt, und plötzlich haben wir das World Trade Center vor uns, gigantisch und doch so simpel wie ein Kinderspielzeug.

Ist hier von einem Film die Rede? Tatsächlich hat das Buch das Tempo eines Films. Menschen, Autos, Gebäude rauschen auf uns zu und an uns vorüber und deuten dabei immer wieder eine Geschichte an. Man betrachtet die riesige menschliche Gestalt, die sich scheinbar auf der Seite eines Wolkenkratzers abzeichnet, als würde sie jeden Moment in ihn einbrechen oder aus ihm herausplatzen, den Schein der Neonlichter, die über den Himmel treibenden Wolken

und wiederum die Twin Towers, die sich in einer Explosion aus gleißendem Licht aufzulösen scheinen. Diese Stadt lebt, pulsiert wie ein Herz, vibriert wie ein Nervensystem, arbeitet wie ein Gehirn.

Noch ein Bild der Twin Towers, aufgenommen durch den Triumphbogen auf dem Washington Square, fragil, als seien sie aus Papier. Daneben ein anderes Foto. Stark und stolz wachsen die beiden Türme empor, anscheinend geradewegs hinauf zum Mond, der in Wirklichkeit ein Lichtreflex der Kamera ist. Dann aber folgt ein Schild mit der Aufschrift NEW YORK – TOUGHEST CITY ON EARTH, auf das Unheil deutend, das "die stärkste Stadt der Welt" treffen wird. Bis ins Mark erschüttert das Bild von Ground Zero, das nun folgt, quälend erinnert es an den Turm zu Babel von Pieter Breughel. Aber diese Türme sind zusammengebrochen, reduziert auf verbogenes Eisen. In einer weiteren, ebenfalls durch den Triumphbogen auf dem Washington Square fotografierten Ansicht sind die Türme verschwunden – man spürt einen seltsamen Widerspruch zu dem friedlichen Treiben. Auf anderen Bildern sind die Schilder zu sehen, die kurz danach wie Blumen aus dem Boden sprossen. Die letzten beiden Fotos zeigen die Freiheitsstatue, geisterhaft und beherrschend zugleich, und ein junges Paar, das Arm in Arm durch das Verkehrsgewühl schlendert, so wie es die New Yorker eben tun. Die Geschichte geht weiter. Das ist die Geschichte.

Aber es gibt noch eine andere. New York zu fotografieren ist schwierig. Nur Paris und Venedig werden so oft in Filmen, im Fernsehen, in der Werbung und auf Postkarten abgebildet wie diese Stadt. Auch für Lensfield eignen sich die Wahrzeichen New Yorks als Motive: das Flatiron Building, gespiegelt in einer Pfütze, das Chrysler Building als verzerrte Reflexion in einem Bürofenster über einem Coca-Cola-Lieferwagen, der Cotton Club in Harlem, die grazilen Statuen des Rockefeller Centers, die kathedralenartige Halle der Grand Central Station. Beim Durchblättern dieser Bilder aber, beim Betrachten der hohen Gebäude, der grellen nächtlichen Lichter und der so verschiedenartigen Gesichter der Passanten fand ich jene Stadt wieder, die mich so gefesselt hatte, als ich vor beinahe einem Vierteljahrhundert hierher zog, die ich aber, wie es mit allem allzu Vertrautem geschieht, nicht mehr wirklich wahrgenommen hatte. Und hier war sie wieder, frisch wie ein Eimer voll Eiswasser ins Gesicht. Genau so zeigt sich New York denen, die es mit neuen Augen sehen.

Anthony Haden-Guest

André Gide a un jour fait remarquer que pour écrire à propos d'un endroit, vous deviez y être depuis deux semaines ou depuis vingt ans. Cela vaut peut-être également pour les photographes. Certains semblent aussi à l'aise avec les scènes qu'ils photographient qu'un tronc abattu dans la forêt ou qu'un prisonnier dans sa cellule. Certains braquent immédiatement leur objectif, comme de nouveaux arrivants, l'œil aux aguets et étonné, embrassant ce qui est familier pour en faire du neuf. Telle est la stratégie de Lance Lensfield.

Or, c'est bien ainsi que les choses doivent être, car « Lance Lensfield » est, effectivement un nouveau venu. Il est l'alter ego de Stefan May, célèbre pour ses clichés sensuels pris en couleur et en noir et blanc à l'aide d'appareils photo de format moyen. Lance Lensfield a vu le jour spécialement pour ce projet : un ouvrage photographique sur New York, immortalisé en noir et blanc à l'aide d'appareils de petit format, comme des Leicas. Il a visité cette ville pour la première fois en 1995, avant d'y revenir chaque année pour quelques jours, une semaine ou deux. C'est ainsi que le livre a pris forme. Puis vint le 11 septembre. Lensfield était confronté à trois choix. Il a jugé impossible d'ignorer l'événement et ce n'était pas de son goût de se concentrer exclusivement sur lui. Nous avons donc ce que nous voyons ici.

Nous commençons à nous pencher avec un certain vertige sur le futurisme suranné du paysage urbain, comme si nous étions à bord d'un petit avion, avant de piquer sur une femme, dont le dos nu luit comme un phoque, tandis qu'elle regarde elle-même vers le bas – depuis une chambre d'hôtel si l'on en juge par le lit défait. Très vite, nous nous trouvons dans une rame de métro, dans une rue qui semble exploser, devant un mélange de citoyens et, brusquement, devant le World Trade Center, aussi énorme et simple qu'un jouet d'enfant.

Est-ce que je donne l'impression de décrire un film ? Pour l'œil, ce livre est rythmé comme un film. Les personnes, les voitures et les bâtiments glissent vers nous et nous dépassent, faisant sans cesse allusion à une histoire. Prenons le visage humain géant qui semble se réfléchir sur le côté d'un gratte-ciel, comme pour y pénétrer, ou pour le faire voler en éclats, et la manière dont les néons fleurissent, dont les nuages flottent, et dont les Twin Towers réapparaissent, explosant en vers de lumière extatique qui se tortillent. Cette ville vit, pompe comme un cœur,

vibre comme un système nerveux, travaille comme un cerveau.

Pourtant, une autre image des Twin Towers les montre évanescentes, comme fabriquées en papier, vues au travers de l'arche sur Washington Square. A côté de cette image s'en trouve une autre. Les tours s'élancent avec confiance, visiblement vers la lune, en fait vers une explosion de lumière créée par l'appareil photo. Mais ensuite, la photo d'un panneau où l'on peut lire NEW YORK – TOUGHEST CITY ON EARTH (New York, la ville la plus dure du monde) est le signe de mauvais augure qui s'impose. Elle précède une photo effroyable de Ground Zero, le lieu de la catastrophe – une image qui présente une ressemblance obsédante avec la Tour de Babel d'un certain Pieter Breughel, mais effondrée et métastasée en ferrailles tordues. Sur une autre photo prise au travers de l'arche de Washington Square – une image dont la charge émotive contraste avec son affairement tranquille – les Twin Towers ont disparu. D'autres photos montrent les panneaux qui ont germé peu de temps après, comme des fleurs. Les deux dernières images du livre montrent la Statue de la Liberté, fantomatique mais dominante, ainsi qu'un jeune couple se tenant par le bras, marchant à grandes enjambées dans la circulation comme le font les New-yorkais. L'histoire continue. C'est ça, l'histoire.

Mais il existe également une autre histoire. Il est difficile de photographier New York – une ville dont les seules rivales sont Paris et Venise pour le nombre de fois où elle apparaît dans des films, à la télévision, sur des publicités ou sur une pléthore de cartes postales. Lensfield a pris des photos de repères – le Flatiron Building, réfléchi dans une flaque d'eau, le Chrysler, qui se reflète dans une fenêtre de bureau au-dessus d'un camion de Coca Cola, le Cotton Club de Harlem, la statuaire débonnaire du Rockefeller Center, le cœur de la Gare centrale, pareil à une cathédrale – mais en feuilletant ces images de bâtiments élevés, de lumières nocturnes brillantes, le kaléidoscope des visages sur les trottoirs, j'ai retrouvé la ville qui m'a exalté lorsque j'ai emménagé ici, voilà près d'un quart de siècle, mais que j'avais cessé de vraiment remarquer, comme cela se produit avec ce qui vous est trop familier. Et maintenant, elle est de nouveau là – fraîche comme un seau d'eau glacée au visage. C'est comme cela que des yeux neufs voient New York.

Anthony Haden-Guest

André Gide observó una vez que, para escribir sobre un lugar, el autor debería permanecer allí durante dos semanas o durante veinte años: Estas palabras probablemente sean válidas también para los fotógrafos. Algunos parecen compenetrarse tanto con las escenas que fotografían como un tronco con la floresta o como un prisionero con su celda. Otros captan sus objetos como recién llegados de ojo avizor y sorprendido, mirando lo familiar y transformándolo en algo nuevo. Ésta es la estrategia de Lance Lensfield.

Y así es exactamente como debería ser: Lance Lensfield es, en efecto, un recién llegado. Es el alter ego de Stefan May, conocido por sus sensuales imágenes, tanto en blanco y negro como en color, tomadas con cámaras de formato medio. Lance Lensfield parece haber nacido específicamente para ejecutar este proyecto: un libro de imágenes de Nueva York, tomadas en blanco y negro mediante cámaras de pequeño formato, como Leicas. Visitó esta ciudad por primera vez en 1995, retornando año tras año por un par de días, por una o dos semanas, y el libro fue tomando forma. Hasta que llegó el 11 de septiembre. Lensfield tenía tres opciones: pasar por alto el suceso, lo que consideró imposible, concentrarse exclusivamente en él, lo que no era de su gusto, o bien presentar el resultado que vemos aquí.

Desde lo alto, como si fuera desde un pequeño avión, nuestra mirada se desliza, vertiginosa, sobre el anticuado futurismo del paisaje urbano; a continuación, se concentra en la espalda de una mujer, tan brillante que parece húmeda. La mirada de la mujer también se dirige hacia abajo, desde una habitación de hotel, a juzgar por la cama sin hacer. Pronto nos encontramos en un metro, en una calle que parece explotar, vemos un popurrí de habitantes y, de pronto, las Torres Gemelas, tan gigantescas y simples como un juguete.

¿No parezco estar describiendo una película? Para este ojo, el libro tiene el ritmo de una película. La gente, los coches, los edificios se deslizan a toda velocidad hacia nosotros y pasan, siempre insinuando una historia. Observemos por ejemplo la gigantesca figura humana reflejada en el flanco de un rascacielos, como si quisiera penetrar en él o salir de pronto, y cómo florecen los carteles de neón, cómo flotan las nubes y la manera en que las Torres Gemelas aparecen de nuevo, envueltas en hilos de luz extática, destellante. La ciudad vive, pulsante como el corazón, vibrante como el sistema nervioso, trabajando como el cerebro.

Una imagen más de las Torres Gemelas las muestra tan etéreas como si fuesen de papel, vislumbradas a través del arco de Washington Square. Junto a esta imagen vemos otra: las torres se encumbran llenas de confianza, aparentemente, hacia la Luna, en realidad, hacia una explosión de luz creada por la cámara. Pero un cartel con la inscripción: NEW YORK – TOUGHEST CITY ON EARTH (Nueva York – La ciudad más recia de la Tierra) resulta adecuadamente ominoso, pues precede a una fotografía de impacto visceral del nivel cero – una imagen con un embrujador parecido a una Torre de Babel de Pieter Breughel, pero caída y transformada en acero retorcido. En otra de las imágenes tomadas a través del arco de Washington Square – una imagen llena de peso en contraste con su pausada actividad – las Torres Gemelas han desaparecido. Las imágenes siguientes muestran los signos que surgieron poco después como si florecieran. En las dos últimas imágenes del libro vemos la Estatua de la Libertad, espectral pero dominante, y una joven pareja de bracete, caminando entre el tráfico como verdaderos neoyorquinos. La historia continúa. Ésta es la historia.

Pero también hay otra historia. Es muy difícil fotografiar Nueva York, una ciudad que sólo puede competir con París y Venecia en cuanto a las veces que la hemos visto en películas, en la televisión, en la publicidad y en incontables postales. Lensfield ha tomado algunas fotografías de puntos de atracción típicos – el edificio Flatiron, reflejado en un charco, el de Chrysler, reflejado cual gota gigantesca en la ventana de una oficina, sobre un camión de Coca Cola, el famoso Cotton Club de Harlem, las elegantes estatuas del Rockefeller Center, el área central de la estación Grand Central, cual si fuera una catedral – pero al hojear este libro y ver estas imágenes de los rascacielos, de las brillantes luces nocturnas, del caleidoscopio de rostros en las aceras, redescubro la ciudad que me había entusiasmado cuando me establecí aquí hace casi un cuarto de siglo, pero a la que había dejado de prestar atención, como solemos hacer con todo lo que nos resulta excesivamente familiar. Y ahora es mía otra vez – fresca como un baldazo de agua helada en el rostro. Así es Nueva York vista con nuevos ojos.

Anthony Haden-Guest

André Gide una volta osservo che per scrivere di un posto vi si dovrebbe stare due settimane o vent'anni, e questo forse vale anche per i fotografi. Alcuni sembrano aver dimestichezza con le scene che fotografano quanto un pezzo di legno con il suolo boschivo o un prigioniero con la sua cella. Altri mirano al proprio bersaglio come novellini, aguzzando stupiti gli occhi, guardando il consueto e rendendolo nuovo. Questa è la strategia di Lance Lensfield.

Proprio come dovrebbe essere, perché Lance Lensfield in realtà è un nuovo arrivato. È l'alter ego di Stefan May, famoso per le sue fotografie sensuali scattate sia a colori che in bianco e nero con fotocamere di medio formato. Lance Lensfield sembrava fatto apposta per questo progetto: un libro fotografico su New York, con foto in bianco e nero, scattate con apparecchi di piccolo formato, come le Leica. Egli visitò per la prima volta la città nel 1995, facendovi ritorno annualmente per un paio di giorni, una settimana, o due settimane, e il libro prese forma. Poi arrivò l'11 settembre. Lensfield aveva tre possibilità. Ignorare l'accaduto sarebbe stato impossibile, decise, e concentrarsi esclusivamente su di esso non era nel suo stile. Il risultato è ciò che vediamo qui.

Iniziamo abbassando vertiginosamente lo sguardo verso l'avvenirismo demodé del panorama cittadino, come fossimo su un piccolo aereoplano, poi piombiamo su una donna, la schiena nuda e lucente come una foca, mentre a sua volta guarda giù – da una camera d'albergo, a giudicare dal letto sfatto. Ed eccoci ben presto in metropolitana, una strada che esplode, il guazzabuglio degli abitanti, e all'improvviso, il World Trade Center, enorme e semplice come il giocattolo di un bambino.

Vi pare ch'io stia descrivendo un film? Da questo punto di vista il libro ha l'andatura di un film. Persone, automobili, edifici balzano verso di noi, e si allontanano, accennando sempre ad una storia. Pensate all'enorme sagoma umana che sembra riflessa sul lato di un grattacielo, come se stesse per farvi irruzione, o per andarsene precipitosamente, e al modo in cui splendono i neon, in cui errano le nuvole e riappaiono le Torri Gemelle, esplodendo in vermi serpeggianti di luce estatica. Questa città vive, pompa come un cuore, vibra come un sistema nervoso, funziona come un cervello.

Eppure un'altra foto mostra le Torri Gemelle evanescenti come fossero di carta, intraviste attraverso l'arco di Washington Square. Accanto a quest'immagine ce n'è un'altra. Le Torri vi si librano sicure, apparentemente alla luce della luna, in realtà a quella esplosiva dell'apparecchio fotografico. Ma poi la foto di un cartello con la scritta NEW YORK – TOUGHEST CITY ON EARTH (New York – la città più dura del mondo) è un presagio azzeccato. Precede una fotografia di Ground Zero da far strizzare le budella, un'immagine che rassomiglia in maniera impressionante alla Torre di Babele di Pieter Breughel, ma caduta, metastatizzata in ferro contorto. In un'altra foto scattata attraverso l'arco di Washington Square – un'immagine che convoglia una carica in contrasto con il suo pacifico andirivieni – le Torri Gemelle sono sparite. Altre foto mostrano i cartelli spuntati poco dopo come funghi. Le ultime due immagini mostrano la Statua della Libertà, spettrale ma dominante, e una giovane coppia, a braccetto, che si fa largo tra il traffico come fanno i newyorkesi. La storia continua. Questa è la storia.

Ma c'è anche un'altra storia. È difficile fotografare New York – una città che rivaleggia solo con Parigi e Venezia per il numero di volte in cui appare nei film, in TV, nelle pubblicità e su una miriade di cartoline. Lensfield ha fatto alcune foto di luoghi adeguatamente emblematici – il Flatiron Building, riflesso in una pozzanghera, il Chrysler, distorto nella finestra di un ufficio sopra un camion della Coca Cola, il Cotton Club di Harlem, l'elegante complesso statuario del Rockefeller Center, lo spazio centrale della Grand Central Station, simile ad una cattedrale – ma sfogliando queste immagini di alti edifici, scintillanti luci notturne, il caleidoscopio dei volti sui marciapiedi, ho ritrovato la città che mi aveva esaltato quando venni a vivere qui quasi un quarto di secolo fa, ma che avevo cessato di notare realmente, come si fa con ciò che ci è troppo consueto. Ed ora rieccola di nuovo – fresca come un secchio di acqua ghiacciata in faccia. È così che New York appare ad occhi nuovi.

Anthony Haden-Guest

"When I despair, I remember that all through history the way of truth and love has always won. There have been tyrants and murderers and for a time they seem invincible, but in the end, they always fall---think of it, *ALWAYS*."

To the brave men & women of the NYFD and NYPD,

NYC LOVES YOU

You have our deepest sympathies, and we are forever grateful to you.

MARE CHI

176½

TAVERN

SORRY,
BATHROOMS FOR
CUSTOMERS
ONLY !!!

B

Z100

AIR CONDITIONED
NO PEDDLERS

CUSTOMERS MUST
BE AT LEAST **21**
YEARS OF AGE TO
DRINK AND **MUST**
POSSESS **VALID**
IDENTIFICATION!!!

WANTED
DEAD OR ALIVE

Osama bin Laden

For mass murder in New York City

I ♥
NY
MORE
THAN
EVER

RE MARTIN

COGNAC

WHERE ITALY'S BEST
PROVE IT

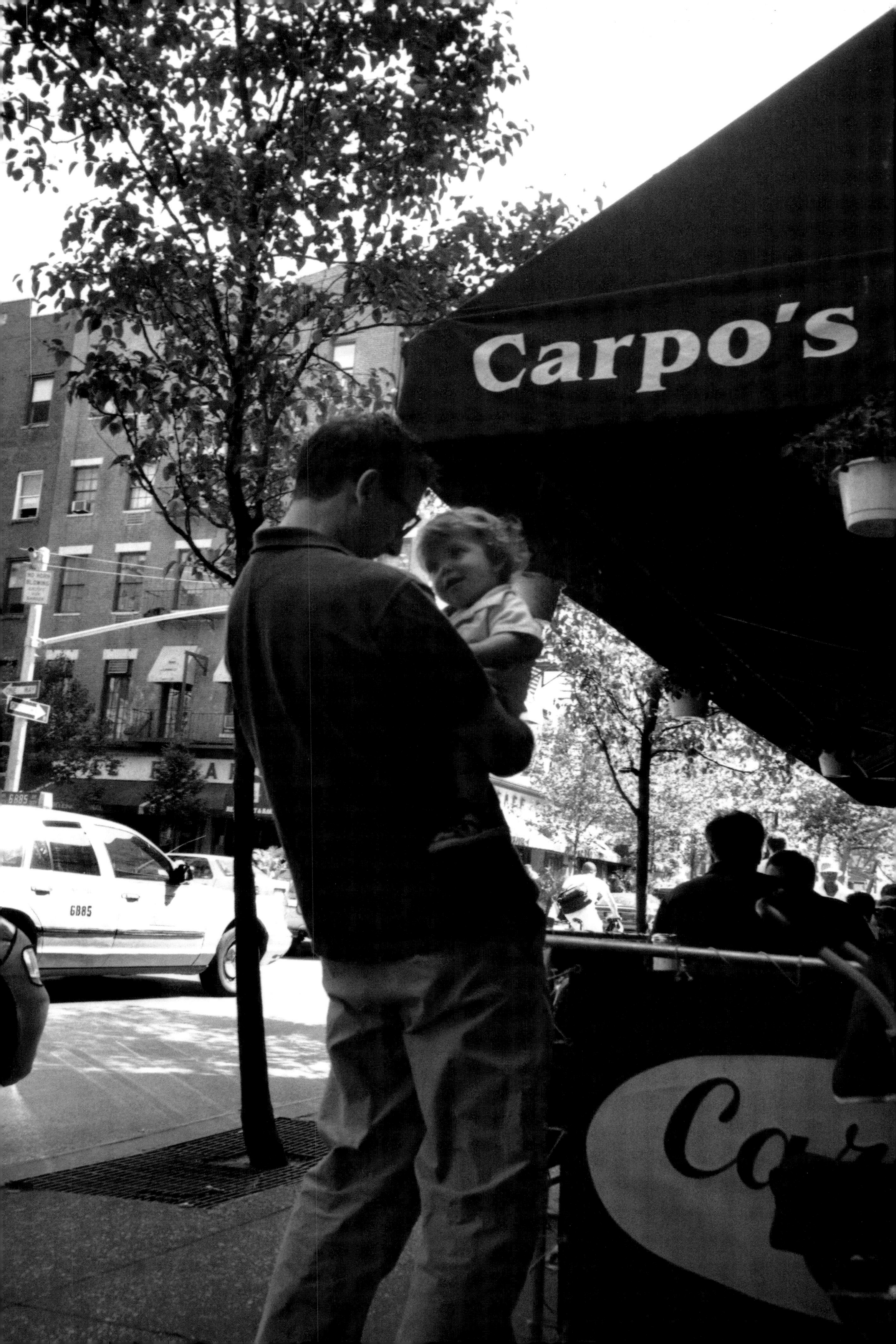
Carpo's

"Skyliner No.2"
Midtown / Murray Hill, 1997

10
"Manhattan No.2"
W 34 ST, Empire State Bld.,
view from Hudson River,
1999

11
"Chelsea"
W 22 ST, Chelsea, 1995

12
"Liberty No.1"
Statue of Liberty, 1997

13
"Stop"
1st AV, Sutton Place, 1997

14
"Love & Peace"
Subway, Brooklyn, 1999

15
"Go"
2nd AV, Sutton Place, 1997

16
"Charging Bull"
Broadway Whitehall / State ST,
Financial District, 2001

17
"Rush Hour No.3"
Madison AV / E 49 ST, 1999

18
"Salesman"
China Town, 1995

19
"Going to Work"
Broadway, Soho, 1995

20
"Big Apple No.2"
Mercer ST, Greenwich Village,
2001

21
"$"
WTC / Financial District,
view from Upper NY Harbour,
1999

22
"Fake Skyliner"
Lexington AV, Midtown, 1999

23
"Faith"
Manhattan / WTC 1,
view from WTC 2, 2001

24–25
"Skyliner 2001"
Manhattan North,
view from top of WTC 2, 2001

26–27
"Skyliner No.1"
Civic Center / TriBeCa / WTC,
view from China Town, 1997